101 Little Known Facts about
KEN GRIFFEY, JR.

Sports Publishing Inc.
a division of Sagamore Publishing
Champaign, IL

© 1997 Dreaming Dog Publishing
All rights reserved.

Book design: Michelle R. Dressen
Cover design: Julie L. Denzer
Cover photo: Allen Kee/Bob Rosato Sports Photography
Photos by Bob Rosato and Allen Kee

ISBN: 1-57167-184-6

Printed in the United States

www.sagamorepub.com

1.
George Kenneth Griffey, Jr. was born November 21, 1969, in Donora, Pennsylvania, the oldest of two boys. He shares the same birthday with Stan Musial (1920), Earl Monroe (1944) and Troy Aikman (1966).

2.
His mother's name is Alberta, but she goes by the nickname "Birdie." His father is Ken Griffey, Sr., who played 19 seasons with four teams in the major leagues. His parents' first date was a high school Sadie Hawkins Dance.

3.
Junior's paternal grandfather, Buddy Griffey, was a high school teammate of Stan Musial in Donora.

4.
As a 16-year-old outfielder, Junior hit three home runs—one to leftfield, one to centerfield and one to rightfield—at the 1986 Connie Mack World Series.

5.
Junior felt so much pressure when his father watched him play that he went hitless in the limited games his father saw from 1982 to '87.

6.
The best advice Ken, Jr., says he got from Ken, Sr., was: "Have fun!"

7.

At Cincinnati Moeller High School, Junior was a star tailback and wide receiver for the football team for three years before sitting out his senior season. His team won the state championship his junior year.

8.
Ken, Jr., was the first player selected in the 1987 major league baseball draft. Ken, Sr., was drafted out of high school in the 29th round of the 1969 draft.

9.
Junior received a bonus of $160,000 from the Seattle Mariners for signing a player's contract right out of high school as a 17-year-old. He was signed by Mariners' scout Tom Mooney.

10.

Ken was assigned to Bellingham, Washington, in the Northwest League. His first hit as a professional was a home run on June 17, 1987, against Everett. He was named the Northwest League Player of the Week with three home runs, eight runs batted in and four stolen bases in his first week.

11.
Ken and his Bellingham teammates traveled on a 1958 school bus that did not have a bathroom. Some of their road trips were 10 hours long.

12.
In January 1988, in a state of depression, Junior swallowed an entire bottle of aspirin. He had to have his stomach pumped at Providence Hospital in Mount Airy, Ohio. He revealed the incident four years later, hoping his admission would help troubled teens.

13.
Ken started his second professional season at San Bernadino in the California League (Class A). Before the season ended, he was promoted to Vermont in the Eastern League (Class AA). In the 129 minor league games in his career, he hit .320 with 103 runs scored, 27 home runs, 92 RBIs, and 49 stolen bases.

14.
As a 19-year-old in the Mariners' 1989 spring training camp, Ken, Jr., batted .359 and had a 15-game hitting streak. He made Seattle's opening day roster and was the youngest player in the majors.

15.
With Ken, Sr., still playing for the Cincinnati Reds, it was the first time a father and son were in the major leagues at the same time.

16.
Ken, Jr., is 6-foot-3, 205 pounds; Ken, Sr., was listed at 5-foot-11, 190 pounds.

17.
Junior was the first player in the majors born after an expansion team won a World Series (the 1969 New York Mets).

18.
In his first major league at bat he doubled off the rightfield wall of Oakland Coliseum against Dave Stewart. In his first at bat in Seattle's Kingdome a week later, his first swing resulted in his first home run, off Chicago's Eric King.

19.
In his first month as a major leaguer, Ken tied a Mariners' record with eight consecutive hits and set a club record by reaching base safely in 11 straight plate appearances.

20.
In his first major league pinch-hit at bat, Ken hit a game-winning two-run homer off Milwaukee's Bill Wegman, May 16, 1989.

21.
Junior hit his first inside-the-park home run against New York, May 21, 1989. He hit his second June 20, 1990, at Kansas City.

22.
He missed a month of his rookie season when he fractured a bone in his right hand after slipping in the shower of a Chicago hotel.

23.
Ken received 79,051 write-in votes for the 1989 All-Star Game. The following year he was voted in as a starter and has been a starter every year since. In 1994 he got a record 6,079,688 votes to break the mark Rod Carew set in 1977.

24.

If Ken remains healthy and productive, he could join about a dozen other players in major league history whose careers spanned four decades. If Griffey plays until 2010, he'll be "just" 40 years old entering his 22nd season. The most recent four-decade players are: Bill Buckner, Rick Dempsey, Carlton Fisk and Nolan Ryan.

25.
Junior led all centerfielders with 10 errors as a rookie, but he also had a league-leading six double plays from the outfield.

26.
In 1989 Ken hit .212 against left-handed pitchers. In 1992 he batted .358 against lefties, the best of any major league left-handed hitter.

27.
As a 20-year-old in the 1990 All-Star Game, Ken was the third youngest player to start in the mid-season classic. Only Al Kaline (in 1955) and Jerry Walker (in 1959) were younger.

28.

After being released by the Cincinnati Reds, Ken, Sr., was signed by the Mariners on August 30, 1990. A day later against Kansas City, Ken, Sr., and Ken, Jr., were side-by-side in the outfield, marking the first time a father and son were in the same line-up.

29.
On September 14, 1990, at California, Ken, Jr., and Ken, Sr., hit back-to-back home runs off Kirk McCaskill.

30.
In 1990, Ken was awarded a Gold Glove for his defensive play. He was the second youngest player to receive the award. Only Cincinnati catcher Johnny Bench in 1968 was younger. Since then, Ken has won the award every season.

31.
Junior has used a Rawlings Trapeze glove since his father gave him that model in 1986. He uses the same glove in practice and games. He goes through four gloves in a season.

32.
Ken uses a Louisville Slugger bat that is 34 inches long and weighs 31 ounces, making it one of the smallest in the big leagues.

33.
In 1991, Ken won a Silver Bat Award as the top hitter at his position, along with his Gold Glove. He and Cal Ripken, Jr., were the only American League players to win both awards that year.

**34.
Ken has won four Silver Bat Awards: 1991, '93, '94 and '96.**

35.
Junior hit his first grand slam home run off New York's Lee Guetterman, July 23, 1991. He has eight career slams.

36.
In Ken's first three seasons he hit more grounders than fly balls (567 to 458). In his next three seasons he hit more flies than ground balls (450 to 361).

37.
After losing records in each of the Mariners' first 14 years, Griffey led Seattle to an 83-79 mark in 1991. Prior to Ken's arrival, the Mariners were 787-1101 (.417). From 1989 through '96, Seattle was 592-636 (.485) with four winning seasons.

38.
Ken, Jr., was named the Most Valuable Player in the 1992 All-Star Game after going 3-for-3 with a home run. Ken, Sr., was the MVP of the 1980 All-Star Game.

39. Junior is hitting .444 (8-for-18) in eight All-Star Game appearances.

40.
Ken set an American League record with 573 consecutive errorless chances by an outfielder from April 16, 1992 to August 8, 1993.

41.
In 1992, Ken swung at the first pitch he saw 109 times in 617 plate appearances. He became more selective with experience. In 1993 he swung at the first pitch 91 times, in 1994 he dropped to 64 and in 1995 he was at 38.

42.
Ken wears uniform No. 24, but he wore No. 30 in honor of his father on **Turn Back the Clock Day in Kansas City, May 21, 1993.**

43.
Junior hit his 100th career home run off Kansas City's Billy Brewer, June 15, 1993. He was the sixth youngest player to reach that mark.

44.
Ken hit his 150th career home run off Texas' Roger Pavlik, May 20, 1994. He was the third youngest player to reach that mark, trailing only Mel Ott and Eddie Mathews.

45.
He hit his 200th career home run off Boston's Vaughn Eshelman, May 21, 1996. He was the seventh youngest to reach that mark. The other six are all Hall of Famers.

46.
He hit his 250th career home run off Toronto's Roger Clemens, April 25, 1997. Despite missing 205 games because of injuries and work stoppage, he was the fourth youngest player to reach that mark. He trailed Jimmie Foxx, Eddie Mathews and Mel Ott.

47.
At the 1993 All-Star Game in Baltimore, Ken became the first player to hit the B & O Warehouse in rightfield when he smacked it during the home run hitting contest, a blast estimated at 460 feet. He finished second in the competition to Texas' Juan Gonzalez, but Ken won the title the following year in Pittsburgh.

48.
Junior tied the major league record with at least one home run in eight consecutive games from July 20 to 28, 1993. He doubled off the wall in Game 9. He tied the mark set by Dale Long in 1956 and matched by Don Mattingly in 1987.

49.
The night Griffey tried to break the consecutive-game home run record, 30,220 tickets were sold the day of the game. That remains a Mariners' walk-up record.

**50.
Ken's longest consecutive-game hitting streak is 12. He's accomplished that four times, the last time in 1993.**

**51.
Ken has been exclusively an outfielder or designated hitter, except for a ninth inning appearance at first base in Minnesota, October 2, 1993.**

52.
In 1993 Ken became the 10th youngest player in major league history to hit 40 or more home runs in a season. He belted 45 that year.

53.
With 40 home runs in 1994, Junior was just the 22nd player in history to record back-to-back 40-homer seasons.

54.
Ken has led the American League in three offensive categories: home runs (40 in 1994), road home runs (24 in 1993) and total bases (359 in 1993).

55.
Ken's only appearance in the minor league's Triple A level was August 13, 1995, at Tacoma on an injury rehabilitation assignment. As a designated hitter, he was 0-for-3 with one strike out.

56.
Ken recorded his 1,000th career hit off Minnesota's Frankie Rodriguez, August 16, 1995, with a first-inning single. He was the seventh youngest player to reach that mark.

57.
Junior's first-ever game-ending hit was August 24, 1995, a ninth-inning two-run home run off John Wetteland to beat New York.

58.
In Seattle's first appearance in post-season play in 1995, Junior hit .364 with six home runs and nine RBI in 11 games. His five home runs in the Divisional Series tied Reggie Jackson's 1977 mark for most HRs in any post-season series and the six tied the most in a post-season (Bob Robertson, '71 Pirates and Lenny Dykstra, '93 Phillies).

59.
Ken hit three home runs in a game for the first time May 24, 1996, against New York. He did it again April 25, 1997, against Toronto.

60.
Junior stole the 100th base of his career June 2, 1996, to become the first Mariner with 100 home runs and 100 stolen bases.

**61.
Led by Ken's 125 runs scored and 140 runs batted in, Seattle averaged 6.1 runs per game in 1996 to become the highest scoring team in the major leagues in 46 years.**

62.
In 1996 Griffey (49 homers) and teammates Jay Buhner (44) and Alex Rodriguez (36) combined to hit 129 home runs, the second best trio in major league history. The only combo better was 143 by Roger Maris (61), Mickey Mantle (54) and Moose Skowron (28) for the '61 New York Yankees.

63.
Junior holds the major league records for most home runs hit by the end of April (13 in 1997), the end of May (23 in 1997) and the end of June (32 in 1994). Roger Maris hit only one home run in April 1961, the year he set the major league record with 61 homers.

64.
Since Maris broke the home run record in 1961, no single-season major league record in any significant hitting category has been broken. That includes batting average, home runs, runs batted in, slugging percentage, runs, hits, singles, doubles, triples, walks and total bases.

65.
Among Ken's tape-measure home runs are: a 462-foot blast into the Kingdome's third deck in 1995; a 460-foot shot in 1993 that hit a speaker hanging from the roof; a 438-foot dinger in 1994 that remains the longest by a left-hander at Camden Yards; and a 1996 cannon that wasn't measured, but landed above the Hard Rock Cafe at Toronto's SkyDome.

66.
Junior has been on the disabled list four times: in 1989 for a fractured little finger on his right hand, in 1992 for a sprained right wrist, in 1995 for a fractured left wrist and in 1996 for a broken hamate bone in his right wrist.

67.
His 1995 wrist fracture—suffered while slamming into an outfield wall—required a three-hour surgery performed by hand specialist Dr. Ed Almquist and Mariner team physician Dr. Larry Pedegana. Ken had a four-inch metal plate and seven screws attached to his left wrist. The plate and screws were removed seven months later.

68.
Junior has a leather recliner with a built-in massager next to his locker stall. He usually takes an hour and a half to dress for a game.

69.
His younger brother, Craig, was a defensive back at Ohio State University and now plays in the Mariners' farm system.

70.
Ken and his wife, Melissa, met at an under-21 alcohol-free club. She asked him to dance.

71.
Ken and Melissa have two children: Trey Kenneth (born January 19, 1994) and Taryn Kennedy (born October 21, 1995). When Trey was born, Mariners' G.M. Woody Woodward sent him a player's contract dated 2012.

72.
Ken and his family have homes in Issaquah, Washington; Cincinnati; and Orlando, Florida. His neighbors in the gated community in suburban Orlando include Tiger Woods, Penny Hardaway, Wesley Snipes and Mark O'Meara.

**73.
Ken still sleeps in the same bed he did as a high schooler in his parents' home.**

74. The Griffey family is the proud owner of three rottweilers.

75.
Ken's first major league contract in 1989 paid him $62,500 a year. That comes to $385 a game for a 162-game season.

76.
In January 1996, Junior signed a contract extension worth $34 million over four years (1997-2000). That comes to $52,469 a game for a 162-game season.

77.
Ken deposited every paycheck from his first four years in the big leagues into a passbook savings account at a Seattle bank.

78.
Junior toured Japan with a group of major league stars in 1990 and '92. He turned down a one-year, $12 million offer to play there full-time.

79.
Ken has endorsement deals worth a reported $5 million in 1997. He does work for Nike (since 1990), Pizza Hut (1996), Nintendo (1992), Upper Deck baseball cards (1990), General Mills/Wheaties (1996), All-Star Cafes (1995), Score Board collectibles (1990), Rawlings (1989) and Gargoyles eyewear (1995).

80.
Despite being allergic to chocolate, Ken had a candy bar named after him in 1989— the Ken Griffey, Jr. Chocolate Bar. More than one million bars were sold.

**81.
Junior was the first baseball player to appear on a box of Honey Frosted Wheaties.**

82.
Ken is a part-owner of the All-Star Cafe chain with Shaquille O'Neal, Andre Agassi, Tiger Woods, Joe Montana and Wayne Gretzky, among others.

83.
The going rate at memorabilia shows for an autographed photo of Ken is $49, an autographed ball is $50 and an autographed bat is $180.

84.
His Fleer rookie card (No. 548) is worth $75 in mint condition or $5 for normal wear. There are nearly 1,000 different card designs that featured him.

85.
In Winter 1996, Nintendo attached more than 15 sensors to Ken to record his body movements and swing to make its games more realistic. There are two Griffey Super Nintendo baseball games on the market and one for Nintendo 64.

86.
Ken has worn Nike spikes since his high school days when his father began wearing them with the New York Yankees. But it wasn't until 1994 that Nike began using Junior in a television ad campaign.

87.
Ken played himself in the movie "Little Big League," filmed in Minnesota following the 1993 season. His one line: "What is Bauer doing? What is he thinking? I might steal third. Just for that, I might steal home." The scene ends with him getting picked off.

88.
Junior has appeared on "The Arsenio Hall Show", "Fresh Prince", "The Simpsons", "Medicine Ball" and "Harry and the Hendersons".

89.
Ken took piano lessons as a child. He worked on a song with M.C. Hammer, but lists Bobby Brown as his favorite singer.

90.
Among Ken's other favorites: Movie—Pulp Fiction; Actor—Samuel L. Jackson; Sport to watch (other than baseball)—Basketball; Sport to play (other than baseball)—Golf; Clothes—Jeans and sweat pants.

**91.
The athlete Junior admired most as a kid was Rickey Henderson.**

**92.
Ken wears a gold "24" on a gold chain around his neck.**

93.
The license plate on one of Ken's cars reads FEAR NO ONE.

**94.
He sold a Ferrari F40 to Reggie Jackson.**

95.
Ken received the 1994 Celebrity Recognition Award from the Make-A-Wish Foundation and the A. Bartlett Giamatti Award from the Baseball Assistance Team in recognition of his "caring for fellow citizens." He also was the 1996 Mariners' Roberto Clemente Award winner for outstanding community service.

96.
Junior's Kids Center provides 200 tickets to every Saturday home game for underprivileged youth. They sit in Section 126 of the Kingdome, directly behind Griffey in centerfield.

97.
Ken has sponsored Christmas Dinner for 350 youngsters from the Rainier Vista Boys and Girls Club every year since 1994. He makes sure every child receives a gift.

98.
When Ken heard 11-year-old Dominique Mayo of Harrisburg, Pennsylvania, on "The Maury Povich Show" say Junior was his only male role model, Ken invited him to a Mariners' game in New York.

99.
Ken authored an "Hey Junior" column in a Seattle newspaper where he answered questions from kids.

100.
Ken is a regular playing partner with Tiger Woods in the off-season. When they play golf, Junior gets spotted 12 strokes by the 1997 Masters champion.

101.
Ken Griffey, Jr., can be reached by writing in care of: Seattle Mariners, P.O. Box 4100, Seattle, WA 98104.

Also available in the *101 Little Known Facts* series:

101 Little Known FACTS about... Michael Jordan

Available at your local bookstore or by calling (800) 327-5557

Also available in the *101 Little Known Facts* series:

Available at your local bookstore or by calling (800) 327-5557

Also available in the
101 Little Known Facts **series:**

101 Little Known FACTS about... Karl Malone

Available at your local bookstore or by calling (800) 327-5557

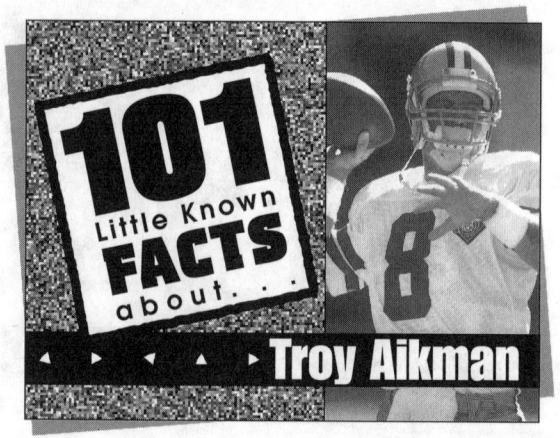

Also available in the *101 Little Known Facts* series:

101 Little Known FACTS about... Troy Aikman

Available at your local bookstore or by calling (800) 327-5557

More titles coming soon in the *101 Little Known Facts* series!

For more information, contact your local bookstore or call (800) 327-5557